Count With Me

CRYSTAL SIKKENS

HOW LONG?

A Crabtree Roots Book

Crabtree Publishing
crabtreebooks.com

School-to-Home Support for Caregivers and Teachers

This book helps children grow by letting them practice reading. Here are a few guiding questions to help the reader with building his or her comprehension skills. Possible answers appear here in red.

Before Reading:

- What do I think this book is about?
    - *I think this book is about length.*
    - *I think this book is about measuring.*
- What do I want to learn about this topic?
    - *I want to learn how to find out if something is longer or taller.*
    - *I want to learn what I can use to measure how long something is.*

During Reading:

- I wonder why...
    - *I wonder why some things are taller and some things are longer.*
    - *I wonder why we use paper clips to measure.*
- What have I learned so far?
    - *I have learned that I don't always need a ruler to measure length.*
    - *I have learned that I can measure to find out how long something is.*

After Reading:

- What details did I learn about this topic?
    - *I have learned that length is how long something is..*
    - *I have have learned I can measure using paper clips.*
- Read the book again and look for the vocabulary words.
    - *I see the word **length** on page 3 and the word **longer** on page 5. The other vocabulary words are found on page 14.*

I want to learn about **length**.

Length is how long something is.

I can see the red pencil is **longer**.

I can see
the gray car
is **shorter**.

I can see the
boy is **taller**.

I can **measure** length.

The blue pencil is five paper clips long.

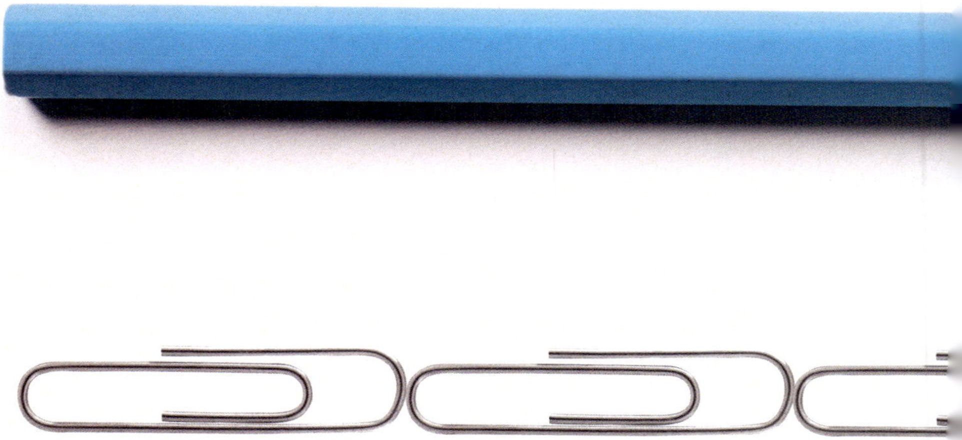

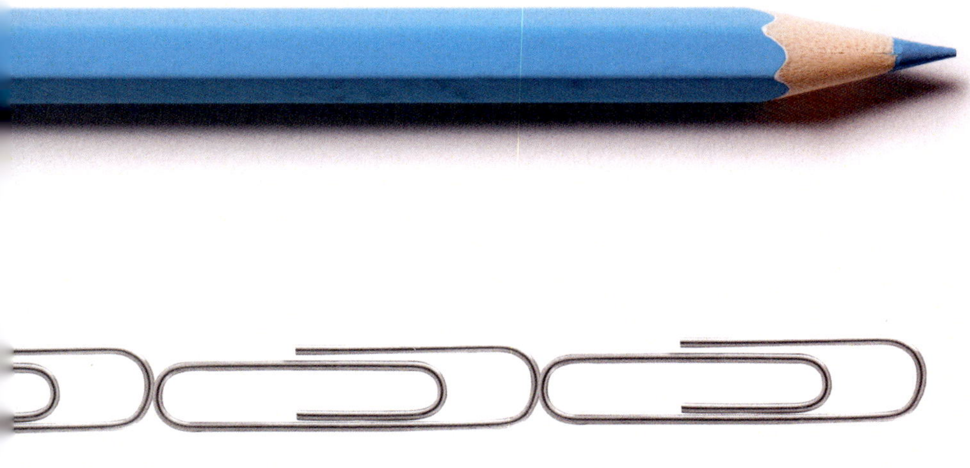

Word List

Sight Words

about	I	see
blue	is	the
can	long	to
how	red	want

Words to Know

length

longer

measure

shorter

taller

47 Words

I want to learn about **length**.

Length is how long something is. I can see the red pencil is **longer**.

I can see the gray car is **shorter**.

I can see the boy is **taller**.

I can **measure** length.

The blue pencil is five paper clips long.

HOW LONG?

Count With Me

Crabtree Publishing

crabtreebooks.com 800-387-7650

In Canada: We acknowledge the financial support of the Government of Canada through the Canada Book Fund for our publishing activities.

Hardcover	978-1-0398-7269-1
Paperback	978-1-0398-7327-8
Ebook (pdf)	978-1-0398-7384-1
Epub	978-1-0398-7433-6

Published in Canada
Crabtree Publishing
616 Welland Avenue
St. Catharines, Ontario
L2M 5V6

Published in the United States
Crabtree Publishing
347 Fifth Avenue
Suite 1402-145
New York, NY 10016

Written by: Crystal Sikkens
Designed by: Margaret Salter
Proofreader: Kathy Middleton
Photographs: Sergey Lavrentev/Shutterstock.com: 6-7 (top). All other images by Shutterstock.com
Production manager: Candice Campbell

Printed in the U.S.A./CP022026